Michael Jordan

By
Dan McCune

CRESTWOOD HOUSE
New York

LIBRARY OF CONGRESS CATALOGING IN PUBLICATION DATA

McCune, Dan
   Michael Jordan
   SUMMARY: A career biography of high-scoring Michael Jordan, basketball player with the Chicago Bulls.
   1. Jordan, Michael, 1963- —Juvenile literature. 2. Basketball players—United States—Biography—Juvenile literature. 3. Chicago Bulls (Basketball team)—Juvenile literature. [1. Jordan, Michael, 1963- 2. Basketball players. 3. Afro-Americans—Biography.] I. Title. II. Series: SCU-2.
GV884.J67M39   1988   793.3'23'0924—dc19   [B]   87-29021
ISBN 0-89686-364-6

International Standard Book Number: 0-89686-364-6

Library of Congress Catalog Card Number: 87-29021

PHOTO CREDITS

Cover: Focus West: (Stephen Dunn)
Focus West: (Rick Stewart) 17, 40, 44, 45, 46; (Stephen Dunn) 18, 24-25
Globe Photos, Inc.: (John Barrett) 27
UPI/Bettmann News Photos: (Paquin) 12; (Neal Hamberg) 33; (Gary Caskey) 36; (Balletti) 39
Sports Illustrated: (Manny Millan) 4, 7, 8, 10, 15, 21, 23, 30-31, 34-35, 38; (Buck Miller) 26, 43

Copyright © 1988 by Crestwood House, Macmillan Publishing Company

All rights reserved. No part of this book may be reproduced or transmitted in any form or by any means, electronic or mechanical, including photocopying, recording, or by any information storage and retrieval system, without permission in writing from the Publisher.

Macmillan Publishing Company
866 Third Avenue
New York, NY 10022
Collier Macmillan Canada, Inc.

Printed in the United States of America
10 9 8 7 6

TABLE OF CONTENTS

Michael Jordan—Superstar 5

A Legend Waiting to Happen 6

College Calls 9

North Carolina's Shooting Star 9

Olympic Gold 11

Rookie of the Year 13

Money For What He Loves to do Most 16

Who Knows Michael Jordan? 19

Sidelined 28

Michael the Mighty 37

King of the Hill 41

A Leap into the Future 47

Michael Jordan's Professional Statistics 48

The amazing Michael Jordan.

MICHAEL JORDAN— SUPERSTAR

He floats. He flies. He soars. In the air, at the top of his shots, he almost proves that what goes up does not *have* to come down. He's Michael Jordan! The number of shots he makes is amazing. He averages more than 37 points per game!

Michael Jordan plays for the Chicago Bulls of the National Basketball Association, and sportswriters call him another Dr. J.

He was just a freshman at the University of North Carolina when he locked up the NCAA championship title for the Tarheels. Twice he was named College Player of the Year. He co-captained the 1984 men's U.S. Olympic basketball team. That team won the gold medal. He was drafted by the Bulls at the end of his third year in college. From the very first, he brought excitement to the basketball court. People poured into arenas to see him play.

And yet, the man behind all the excitement is low-key. He cleans his own house. He does his own laundry. He remembers things like Halloween trick-or-treats for the kids in his neighborhood. And when the Illinois-Indiana car dealers gave him his choice of any kind of car, he drove away in a four-wheel drive vehicle. It would help him get around in the snow, he said.

Where did he come from, this man who at the age of 21 conquered pro basketball?

A LEGEND WAITING TO HAPPEN

Michael Jeffrey Jordan was born February 17, 1963, in Brooklyn, New York. Later, his parents moved their family to Wilmington, North Carolina. The family was not rich, but they were comfortable. Michael's father, James, was an equipment supervisor at a large factory. His mother, Deloris, was a supervisor at a bank.

Michael is the fourth of five children. His brothers are James and Larry. His sisters are Deloris and Rosylyn.

Michael spent a lot of time playing basketball at Empie Park, a playground in Wilmington. When he wasn't playing, he was waiting to get on the court. Empie Park was not all that big, and there were lots of kids who wanted to play basketball. There was a lot of waiting time, so once he got his turn on the court, Michael had to keep winning to keep his place there.

As a freshman at Laney High School, Michael was too small to make the first team. But basketball was his game. He loved it and played constantly. The games were one-on-one, usually with his brother Larry. He improved steadily. He handled the ball with growing skill. And he sank more and more baskets.

While he was building his skill, he was growing. That helped. He grew from 5′11″ to 6′3″ in the summer before his junior year. When he went back to school in the fall, he was picked for the team.

People began to watch Michael Jordan and to talk about

When No. 23 moves down court, he's in total control.

Michael's jump shots seem effortless.

him. They noticed how well he handled the ball and how he was able to shoot from almost anywhere on the court. And there did seem to be something unusual about the way he jumped when he was shooting...

Michael was making a name for himself as a high school player. He was "someone to watch." People talked about him as "promising." By the time he graduated from Laney High, Michael was one of the most sought-after players of the year.

COLLEGE CALLS

Michael decided to attend the University of North Carolina at Chapel Hill, in his home state. The coaches and the students were excited. But was Michael excited? To know Michael is to understand that he's never satisfied while there is room for improvement. His game could be better, and he knew it. He wasn't perfect. Not yet.

He practiced with the team, of course. But he also practiced on his own. And when he wasn't practicing, he was playing in pick-up games. Coach Dean Smith later said that his progress that first year was "almost eerie."

NORTH CAROLINA'S SHOOTING STAR

The year was 1982. Michael Jordan was a freshman. The University of North Carolina was playing Georgetown University for the National Collegiate Athletics

Who says you can't defy gravity?

Association (NCAA) championship. The Tarheels had Michael Jordan. The Georgetown Hoyas had Patrick Ewing.

The two teams were well-matched and the game was tight. Then in the last seconds Michael set fire to the game. Seeming to come out of nowhere, he placed a dazzling 16-foot jump shot neatly in the basket. The buzzer sounded. That shot clinched the NCAA title for the Tarheels. And it put Michael Jordan in the national spotlight.

The next morning, sportswriters around the country wrote about that amazing jump shot. Here was an athlete with star quality. If young Michael Jordan could play like that in his first year of college ball, what would he do in the years to come? Where would he take the Tarheels in the future?

The next morning, sportswriters wrote about this exciting new star. But Michael Jordan seemed unaffected by his new status. He went back to the campus and played in a pick-up game!

OLYMPIC GOLD

Michael was named to the NCAA All Tournament Team at the Final Four as a freshman at North Carolina. At the close of his sophomore year, he was named College Player of the Year. Those were big honors for the good-natured college student who spent all his spare time bouncing a basketball around with anyone who would play with him. But the honors were just hints of bigger things to come.

The Pan American games are held every four years. The games are an Olympic-style sports event. The nations of North America, Central America, South America, and the Caribbean compete. Michael Jordan had finished his sophomore year at Chapel Hill in 1983, a Pan Am year. He was chosen to play on the U.S. basketball team. He traveled to Caracas, Venezuela, for the games. He was the top scorer, and the U.S. team brought home the gold medal.

Michael celebrates the U.S. victory at the '84 Olympics.

In March 1984, the Tarheels took the NCAA championship a second time. Michael was again named College Player of the Year. 1984 was also an Olympic year. The games would be held in Los Angeles. Not only was Michael picked for the U.S. team, he co-captained it. It was an excellent team, coached by Bobby Knight. Georgetown's Patrick Ewing was on the team. So was Oklahoma's Wayman Tisdale.

Much has been said of Michael's Olympic play. Fernando Martin of Spain had a little trouble with English. But he described Michael simply and well: "Jump, jump, jump. Very quick. Very fast. Very, very good. Jump, jump, jump."

The coach of the Spanish team just shook his head. "He's not human. He's a rubber man." Michael averaged 17.1 points, and the U.S. team carried away the gold medal.

ROOKIE OF THE YEAR

Michael Jordan would have been a senior at North Carolina in the fall of 1984. He had been a good student there, holding a B average in his studies. Sportswriters had predicted he would be named College Player of the Year for the third time in his senior year. But Michael decided to put his studies on hold. He did not go back to Chapel Hill. Instead he decided to become a professional.

Professional basketball had been in a slump for several years. It was just beginning to brighten up in 1984. It got a big boost from an outstanding group of young college players who signed up that year. The group included Akeem Olajuwon, Sam Bowie — and Michael Jordan.

The Houston Rockets had first pick in the college draft. They chose seven-foot Akeem Olajuwon. The Portland Trailblazers had the number two pick. They went for a tall man, too. They signed Kentucky's 7'1" Sam Bowie. The Chicago Bulls must have been rubbing their hands, smiling and waiting. Michael Jordan was theirs!

The Bulls had had a terrible few years. They made the championship playoffs only once in seven years. That was 1980-1981. Spirit on the team was low. As one sportswriter put it, the players almost expected to lose. Attendance was bad. But now they had an attraction, and they knew it. The Bulls took ads in the Chicago newspapers to tell the world about signing Michael.

Chicago opened its arms to Olympian Michael. Ticket sales zoomed. Great things were expected of him. Everybody wanted to be there to see. The pressure on Michael must have been tremendous. He was moving to a new town and starting a new life. And in his first pro season he was supposed to turn a losing team into a winner.

As a college player, Michael had played under college rules. The rules in the NBA were more open, and timing would be somewhat different. The NBA rules give players greater freedom. Michael could open up his game in this new set-up. And open up he did.

His shots were magical. The ball rolled easily off his fingers. He seemed to hang over the basket and dropped in the balls. The crowds loved him. They roared with delight.

Dunk shots are routine with Michael.

The 17,000-seat Chicago Stadium sold out during home games. So did arenas at out-of-town games.

People began to expect him to pile up the scores. In his first weeks with the team, he showed what he could do. He averaged 27 points a game. He pulled the team along with him toward the top of the league's Central Division.

In November, he led the Bulls to victory over the San Antonio Spurs, scoring 45 points. He was named starting guard on the Eastern All-Star team. In New York, he made 33 points in a winning game against the Knicks. A crowd of 19,000 people watched.

Michael found surprisingly friendly crowds on the road. People came out of curiosity. They watched him in wonder. They were good-natured about seeing their teams lose. At least they were losing to a top-ranked player!

Michael's season high was a staggering 49 points against the Detroit Pistons. It was the most points ever scored by a Chicago Bull rookie in a single game.

At the end of his first season in the league, he had scored more points than any other player in the NBA — 2,213. Michael was named Rookie of the Year.

MONEY FOR WHAT HE LOVES TO DO MOST

Michael was given a five-year contract when he signed with the Bulls. It guaranteed him $4 million over five years. That amounted to $800,000 a year. The contract wasn't as big as those of some of the big names in the game. For instance, Larry Bird plays for more money. But, Larry has been around for a while. Michael was just starting out.

There was something to think about besides the basketball contract: tie-ins with companies that wanted him to promote their goods. Michael signed a contract with

Nike for five years. Shoes and clothing would carry his name. Wilson Sporting Goods signed him to a three-year contract. Other companies were quick to jump onto the Michael Jordan bandwagon.

The offensive drive never stops when Michael takes possession.

There is something most unusual about Michael's contract with the Bulls. He asked for something no other player had. He wanted the right to play anywhere with anyone in the off-season. He might even play for free. The owners grumbled. They were taking a chance on this newcomer. If he played in unscheduled games, he might get hurt.

But that's the way Michael felt about the contract and about the game. He loves basketball. He needed to feel he could play when he felt like it.

He got the clause. It's called his love-of-the-game clause. He plays in pick-up games, and he likes to drop in on unofficial college games. One young player recalls such a game. His favorite moment came when Michael blocked his shot!

WHO KNOWS MICHAEL JORDAN?

At 6'6" and 195 pounds, Michael is the very picture of a superb athlete. He has the shoulders of a football player, the strong legs of a distance runner, and the grin of a boy. His manner is more than polite, it is gracious. He makes it easy for strangers to talk to him. And everybody wants to. He is good-natured about signing autographs and talking with kids.

Free throws allow players to catch their breath.

All the people who watch him play feel as though they know him. Young fans pay him the biggest compliment of all — they imitate him. They lace their shoes only to the second eyelet from the top, because that's the way Michael does his shoes. Some kids have gone so far as to adopt his stuck-out tongue style of play. Michael has warned them about that, though. They could bite their tongues, he says.

Players and coaches know other sides of Michael Jordan. They admire his talent for stacking up points. He's one of the great players, and they know it.

Michael had not been with the Bulls very long when Coach Doug Collins pointed out that Michael was "one terrific guy." If that weren't true, he said, the other players would not be so willing to work with him.

After a mind-boggling 63-point game, Dennis Johnson of the Boston Celtics said, "No one was guarding him. No one *can* guard Michael Jordan."

Larry Bird joked, "Maybe he's God disguised as Michael Jordan."

But there is more to this man than what fans and players see. He hates to lose. That was true even back in his college days. His teammate and friend Buzz Peterson said that Michael hated to lose at any game, whether it was cards or pool or basketball. That meant he was determined to get a lot better at playing basketball.

He finishes what he starts. We know that about him, too. He set out to play basketball, the best basketball. He does just that!

And he also cleans his own house. That tells a lot about

Whenever Michael goes up for a shot, his tongue leads the way.

Michael Jordan. He has been firm about it and has told people he does not need anyone to help him. The home economics classes he took back at Laney High have been a big help. He scrubs the place down and keeps it looking good.

Other things he learned as a kid growing up in Wilmington have stuck. While he was still at home, his parents warned him about drugs and alcohol. He has remembered.

And then there's that trick with his tongue. That definitely came from home. He saw his father doing that when he was working on some job around the house, or on the family car. Michael picked up the habit. He can't break it. Coach Dean Smith at North Carolina tried to help him. No luck. The tongue comes out when he's thinking hard about what he's doing — like going for a basket.

So this is what Michael Jordan tells about himself through his actions. He shows that he is a determined winner, a perfectionist, a man who keeps his goals in sight, someone who finishes what he starts.

Michael also has a temper, and he's been known to lose it. When a player from an opposing team began a shoving match, Michael looked surprised at first. He let it pass. But when the same player tried that again, Michael blew his cool. The referees had to hold him back.

At 6'6" and 195 pounds, Michael makes an awesome opponent.

Sometimes, Michael and the referees don't see eye to eye.

Michael enjoys a friendly game of pool with his father, James.

"Mr. Jordan" steps out.

SIDELINED

Hopes were high as the 1985-1986 season opened. Michael had proved himself as a rookie. Would there be any stopping him this season? Would he set new records? And how would the Bulls do?

The first two games promised good things to come. Michael led the Bulls to a win over Cleveland. He scored 29 points. The next game was even more exciting. Michael scored 33 points and the Bulls took the Detroit Pistons.

And then came October 28, 1985.

The Bulls were playing their third game at Golden State. Halfway through the game, Michael came down hard on his left foot.

At first the doctors thought the problem was not serious. Athletes hurt themselves often. Usually injuries are not serious, even though they are painful. This time, tests proved the doctors wrong. X-rays showed Michael had broken a bone in his foot.

The bone needed time to heal. The doctors said there was to be no playing, no practice. The Bull management agreed with the doctors. They could not risk more damage to their star guard's foot. They gave Michael orders to take things easy.

Michael sat on the sidelines and steamed. The Bulls limped along without him. For the first time in his basketball career he was out of action. He had never missed a game before. November passed, and December, and January. The doctors checked his foot often. They said the bone was healing slowly.

At last Michael had had enough. He could not just sit and watch his team without playing. He packed his bags and went back to Chapel Hill. Everyone thought he had gone back to North Carolina to work on his degree. But that wasn't how things turned out.

Michael began to feel good. His foot was hurting less and less. He thought he knew his own body better than anybody else did, and his body seemed to be telling him that his foot was okay. He began to play in pick-up games.

But word got back to the Bulls. What in the world was Michael Jordan doing there in North Carolina? Playing basketball? That was against doctors' orders! They called him back to Chicago in a hurry.

More tests were made. The doctors shook their heads. There was a 10 percent chance the bone could break again if Michael put stress on it. The doctors told him to sit out the rest of the season and let the bone heal. The Bulls agreed with the doctors. They told Michael he was out of the game until the beginning of the next season.

Michael's stubborn streak came out. He dug in his heels. What was everyone talking about? If there was a 10 percent chance he could break the bone again, then there was a 90 percent chance he would *not* break it. He pointed out that 90 percent made mighty good odds. Who wouldn't take a chance if they had 90 out of 100 chances of winning?

Michael was stubborn. So were the Bulls. Finally both sides gave a little and got a little. The Bulls said Michael could start playing again — but only part time. Michael

On the bench, Michael fidgets until he's back on the court.

agreed to that. Part time playing the game he loved was better than no time.

He suited up and returned to the game in March, 1986. Michael had missed 64 games of the season. Michael's months on the sidelines showed in those first games. He was rusty. At first he only played seven minutes during each half. The time stretched out with each game that followed. But he began to put things back together. In the last ten games of the season, he averaged 26.5 points. The Bulls made it to the final playoffs in the Eastern Conference.

Michael had his game in hand when the Bulls met the Celtics in Boston Gardens. He scored 49 points in the opening game! The second game took place on April 20. There was a full house — almost 15,000 people. They had come to watch Larry Bird and to see Chicago's fantastic Michael Jordan. That's when Michael set a record for the NBA playoffs. He scored 63 points!

A little stubbornness pays off, sometimes.

One-on-one in basketball provides constant excitement during the game.

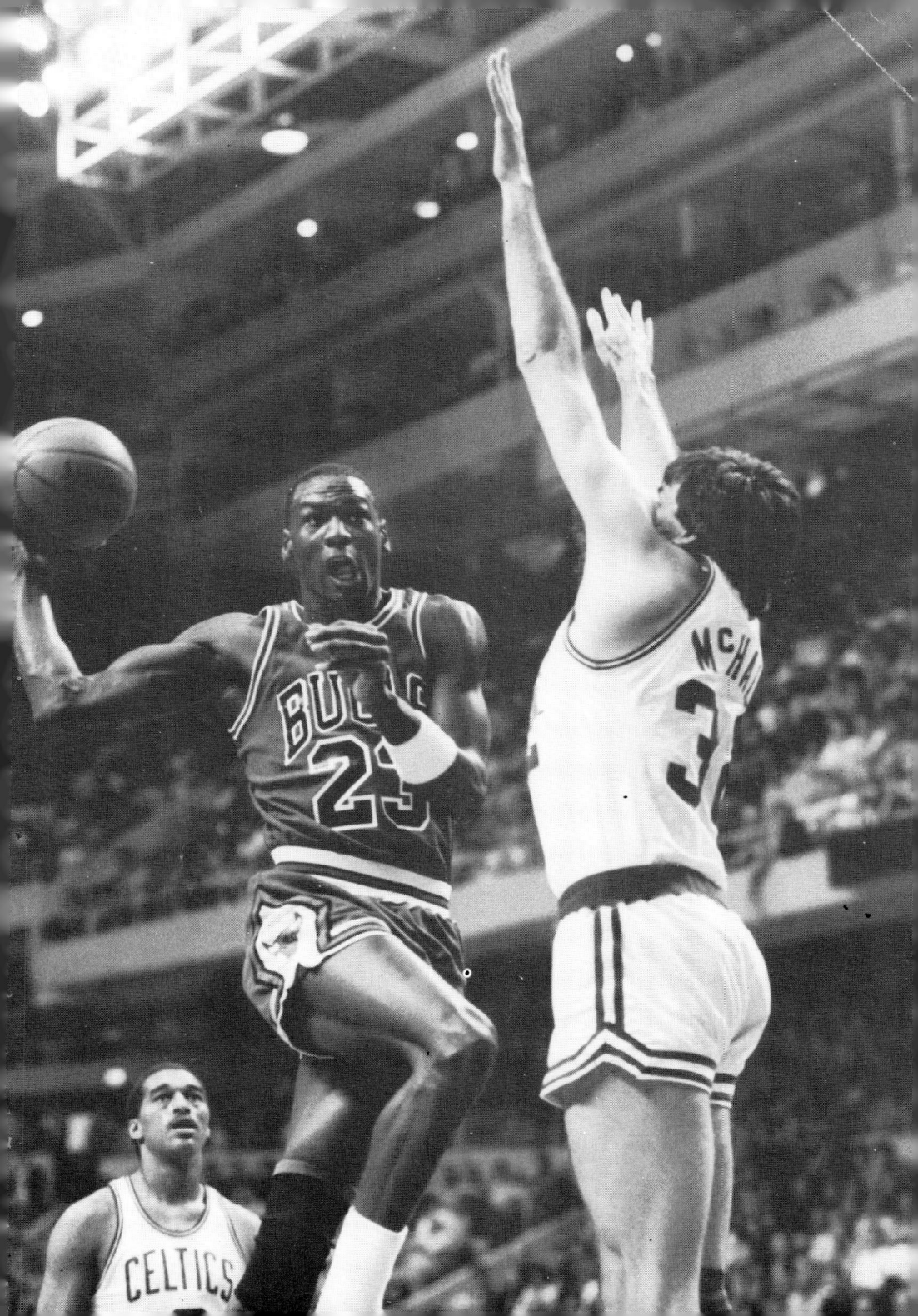

Michael makes nearly all of his free throw attempts.

MICHAEL THE MIGHTY

Michael opened the 1986-1987 season in great shape. He scored 50 points in the opening game. The rest of the season more than lived up to that promise. He nudged records left and right. Or he knocked them over.

He led the league in scoring after that 50-point opening game. No one was able to catch up to him. He ended the season with an average of just over 37 points per game.

In two games he scored 60 or more points.

He scored 50 or more points in three games in a row. Only Wilt Chamberlain has done that.

Playing against Atlanta, he scored 23 points *in a row*.

He had more than 200 steals and 100 blocked shots — another record. He is the first player in NBA history to do that.

He is only the second player in NBA history to go over 3,000 points in one season. The first player was Wilt Chamberlain.

Michael closed the season by being named to the All-Star NBA team, along with Magic Johnson, Akeem Olajuwon, Larry Bird, and Charles Barkely. That's some company!

Nobody dunks the basketball quite like this.

The height of Michael's leaps leaves fans astounded.

Jumping helps maintain a great defense, too.

KING OF THE HILL

In his first three years with the Bulls, Michael has slowly let more of himself show, both on and off the court.

He said he never practices the fantastic stuff that makes people gasp. How could he! He doesn't know when something special will be called for, or what that move will be. He has a quick mind and a body that can follow.

And those leaps! Watching him, you might think he has springs in his legs. He just has wonderfully developed muscles, of course. They carry him high. Even *he* is sometimes surprised at how high. But there's no explanation for his "hang time." That puzzles even him. He has said that when he jumps, he spreads his legs. Maybe that slows him down a little, like a parachute helping him float to earth.

Tie-in contracts with big companies tripled his playing salary by the end of his third year. He set up his own company to handle things, Jordan Universal Marketing Productions. The initials are JUMP. He made his mother and father vice-presidents of the company.

He has been generous with the money he has earned. There is the check he wrote for $15,000 after he visited a children's hospital. And what did he do with the $12,000 in prize money he won in the slam-dunk contest at the 1987 All-Star game? He wrote twelve $1,000 checks and passed them out to his teammates!

This player loves competition!

It's a little harder to get near him for an autograph. The crowds close in around him. Often he has to be surrounded by police to get in and out of airports and hotels. But fans who meet him find that he is still good-natured about signing autographs. And they find that he still does not like being called "Mr. Jordan." "Michael" is just fine.

He still finishes what he starts. He set out to get an education, back in 1981. It took a little longer than he expected. But he did it. After two years in the league, he went back to the University of North Carolina and got his degree in geography.

He admits that he reacts to the cheers of the crowds and plays better when he feels people are rooting for him. It would be easy for him to sit back and enjoy life. But he's still a perfectionist. At home he studies tapes of the games. There's always room for improvement, you know.

It's hard to imagine Michael Jordan needing improvement! But the fact is, he's king of the hill now. Plenty of players in the future are going to try to bump Michael Jordan off the hilltop. They are going to match his play. They are going to challenge his records.

And so Michael keeps on working at his game.

Signing autographs is part of the fun of being a superstar.

Basketball is a sport of speed and pressure.

Michael concentrates on every shot.

A LEAP INTO THE FUTURE

He started out by being compared to the great Julius Erving. Not only did he have skills that were like Erving's, he brought the same excitement to the game.

Three years into the game, his name was being placed beside the great Wilt Chamberlain's. He was challenging Wilt's records.

A good guess, though, is that Michael Jordan will not be a carbon copy of Erving or Chamberlain. Michael Jordan is his own man, with his own style. He has astonishing abilities. Equally important, he has heart for the game. Quite simply, he loves it.

There are records to challenge—other players' records and his own. He will have to keep topping his past records. The lid is off in the NBA. Who knows where Michael Jordan will take basketball in the years to come?

Another point is about to be made for the Chicago Bulls.

MICHAEL JORDAN'S PROFESSIONAL STATISTICS

The Chicago Bulls

1986-1987

Games Played	82
Field Goals Made	1,098
Field Goals Attempted	2,279
Percentage	.482
Free Throws Made	833
Free Throws Attempted	972
Percentage	.857
Rebounds	430
Assists	377
Steals	236
Blocked Shots	125
Points	3,041
Average	37.1